Aryan Books International
New Delhi

Nabakalebara of Lord Jagannath

A.K. Pattanayak

Nabakalebara of Lord Jagannath

ISBN: 978-81-7305-545-4

Published in **2015** by
Aryan Books International
Pooja Apartments, 4B, Ansari Road, New Delhi - 110 002
Tel.: 23287589, 23255799; Fax: 91-11-23270385
E-mail: aryanbooks@gmail.com
www.aryanbooks.co.in

Designed and Printed in India by
ABI Prints & Publishing Co., New Delhi

Writer's Note

Writing on any aspect of Lord Jagannath has always been a fascination for the scholars and more so for the students of history. As such, a lot has already been written on Jagannath and yet there is scope for a lot more. The vastness of Jagannath culture attracts scholars as well as the readers to know more and more about it and from different angles. However, the activities inside the temple are out of bounds even for the serious scholars.

Nabakalebara is an unusual aspect of Jagannath worship. Most part of it takes place inside the temple to which no one, not even the Puja Panda of the temple, has access nor do we have any base record for reference. Major part of the Seva is based on unwritten records and performed on personal experience as secret Nitis. The sources that describe different Nitis maintain stoic silence on Nabakalebara or give a passing reference. Normally, the *Madala Panji*, Utkal Khanda of *Skanda Purana*, *Purusottam Mahatmya*, different Puranas, *Kapila Samhita*, *Niladri Mohadaya*, etc. describe the various Nitis of the temple. All of them are silent about Nabakalebara for some reason or the other. Even the Record of Rights of the Jagannath Temple, which officially regulates all the activities inside the temple, is very brief on Nabakalebara. Only a small paragraph has been devoted for the entire thing. Hence, writing an authoritative and informative book on Nabakalebara is a difficult task.

The next Nabakalebara is due to be held in 2015. The common people are generally curious to know the details about it. Hence, it is the bounden duty of the scholars to make lucid reading books available to them. This is a humble attempt in that direction. It is neither claimed to be either the first or the best. There have been a few works on the topic both in Odia as well as in English. Yet, more the merrier. Since the scope of the work is limited and the area of operation is restricted, there is bound to be similarities in description with the existing works. There is no escape from that. I have avoided technical details of different Pujas and the description of individual Nabakalebaras, and have restricted myself to general principles that regulate things.

It is intended to make it a pictorial coffee-table book without any claim of being authoritative but certainly with correct information. In the process, it was discovered that photos on Nabakalebara are very rare, as most part of it is conducted inside the temple precincts, which is out of bounds of the photographers. The last Nabakalebara was held way back in 1996. Back then, photography had its own limitations and the persons concerned were not conscious of its importance.

In the process of gathering information, I have consulted the works of some worthy scholars, like Dr. G.C. Tripathy, Dr. P.C. Mishra, Sri Mahimohan Tripathy and Dr. Bhaskar Mishra, who have written on Nabakalebara in some form.

I have received help from different sources without which probably things could not have been possible. The help and assistance of Sri Biswanath Samantra, a Badu Suar himself, is invaluable. As a part of the system and a scholarly person, he has provided intellectual, physical and moral support for the work, ungrudgingly. As a matter of fact it, was he who encouraged me to write a book on Nabakalebara. I thank Sri Mahimohan Tripathy, a fine gentleman, who has worked as a part of the temple administration for about a decade and as the Chief Executive-cum-Administrator for more than four years for kindly going through the script and for offering valuable suggestions. I thank Sri Rama Chandra Das Mahapatra, the present Majhi Bada, for kindly having a long discussion with me in this regard. I thank Sri Pradeep Kumar Panda, who is like my son, for the physical and moral support. He has taken all the pain in transferring it to black and white. I am thankful to Prof. Sadasiba Pradhan, Professor, AIHC&A, Utkal University for his association with the project from the very beginning.

I am indebted to my wife and children for their all-round support and encouragement, without which it could not have been possible to complete it.

I am grateful to Mr. Vikas Arya of Aryan Books International, New Delhi for publishing the book elegantly and on time.

Bhubaneswar, 2014

Prof. A K Pattanayak
Former Vice Chancellor
Utkal University of Culture

Nabakalebara of Lord Jagannath

Nabakalebara is one of the grandiloquent events associated with the Jagannath temple of Puri. It is a unique Hindu religious festival in many respects, which is beyond normal human perception. Nabakalebara literally means—*Naba* or new and *Kalebara* or body—new body. The new images take the place of old images and the old images are discarded and buried under the ground. This is Nabakalebara for Jagannath, the Lord (*Natha*) of the Universe (*Jagata*) or the Lord of the Universe, (*Biswa jasya Sri Anga*).

In conformity with the belief that Lord Jagannath is truly a 'Living Deity' with an astonishingly ingenuous human touch, He moves through the life cycle of death and birth sequences shedding His old body and getting into the new one in a remarkably unique and mystic ceremony. Like all mortal human beings, Lord Jagannath brushes teeth, takes bath, eats, sleeps, indulges in pleasure, changes dress, suffers from illness, goes for rest or convalescence, hankers for relations, undertakes travel, goes for seasonal food and social festivals and also like one and all changes his mortal frame. All the fairs, festivals, *bhoga* system, dress habits and other associated things have been so arranged to find human character in Lord Jagannath, who is the Lord of the universe but at the same time a friend, a philosopher and a guide for the devotees. In the *Srimad Bhagavata*, it has been said that if someone takes birth in this world, he is destined to die even if he is a God (*Martya Mandale deha bahi Debata helebi marai*). This stanza of *Bhagavata* has direct reference to Lord Jagannath, as no other God in the Hindu pantheon goes through the birth and death sequence.

The soul is immortal but the human form or the body is temporary. Hence, if the human beings go through the process of change of mortal form and change bodies, how can the God lag behind? The event involves installation of new images as well as the burial of the old ones in the Koili Baikuntha, inside the temple complex by following a well-defined ritualistic procedure.

1. An overview of Sri Mandir.

The *Srimad Bhagavata Gita* (Verse – 22, Chapter II) mentions:

Vasamsi Jirnani yatha vihaya
Navani grahanti naro parani
Tatha sarirani vihaya jirnay
Anyani samyati navani dehi

As a person puts on a new garment, giving up old ones, the soul similarly also accepts new material body giving up the old ones.

This philosophical view is also applicable to the Lords as well. The Lords accept new material form, giving up the old ones.

Nabakalebara, therefore, is a periodic and total replacement of the four images—the *Chaturdha Murty* of Jagannath, Balabhadra, Subhadra and the *Sudarshana*—which according to L.S.S.O' Malley makes it a "rarer festival" (*Bengal District Gazetteers-Puri,* 1908).

The wood as a perishable material is subject to natural decay. Hence, the idols made of wood must undergo replacement or repair from time to time. Images of the Hindu gods and goddesses are made of different materials, which have different periods of longevity. Images can be earthen (*mrunmaya*), painted (*rekha*), wooden (*daru*), metal (*dhatu*), gem (*mani*) and stone (*sila*). The period needed for

2. Panoramic view of Sri Mandir.

the renewal of such images has been prescribed in the *Bhubana Prakash* as one month, one year, twelve years, one thousand years and ten thousand years, respectively. The idols of Lord Jagannath, Balabhadra and Subhadra being made of *Daru,* their longevity as per the scriptures is 12 years.

In case of *Daru Brahma*, the idols can neither be changed as and when required nor can one wait till the images face complete decay. This has to go through a well-defined procedure and fixed time. The renewal takes place between 8 years and 19

3. The *Simha Dwara* (Lion Door) and the *Aruna Stambha*.

years, though it is normally believed that the Nabakalebara takes place after every 12 years. Hence, in a way, the Nabakalebara ceremony is an unavoidable consequence of the fact that the idols being made of wood undergo lots of wear and tear because of the ritualistic pouring of water during the *Snana Purnima* every year and the associated manoeuvering of the idols during the *Ratha Yatra* and *Snana Yatra*. Unlike other gods, the four idols move out twice a year in their original form, during the *Snana Purnima* and the *Ratha Yatra*, which involve lots of wear and tear for the idols. The *Pahandi Bije* or the movement of the idols in and out of the temple on these two occasions year after year, ought to cause serious damage to the idols as such. Considering the size of the idols, the *Pahandi* naturally involves lots of manoeuvering. Since the weight of *Sudarshana* and Subhadra are less, these two are carried on the shoulders by the *Daitapatis*. The idols, of Jagannatha and Balabhadra being unwieldy and very heavy, it is not possible to carry them on shoulders. Hence, they are literally dragged on the floor in standing position by tying ropes all around and by balancing them.

It is another thing as to why the idols have been made of wood, which is perishable. Metal or stone could have been used to give it longer life. The rulers, who constructed such a gigantic and architecturally beautiful temple, made elaborate arrangement for the *Chatishanijoga* (thirty-six different types of *sevas*) and the *Chapanpauti* (fifty-six different types of *Bhoga* system), could have safely carved the images out of metal, gem or even stone. Neither the cost nor the technical knowhow stood as a hindrance. Some other

Top:
4. The *Snana Yatra* – Pouring of water on the idols.

Bottom:
5. The idols on the *Snana Mandapa*.

6. The *Baisi Pahacha* and the *Kurma Dwara*.

extraneous religious factors determined things. As such, the *Chalanti Pratimas* (movable idols) of the deities are made of metal for which these are never changed or replaced. Only the four worshippable idols, made of wood, are replaced.

Numerous theories have been given by different authorities to justify the wooden structure. According to the *Brihat Samhita*, the worship of wooden idols gives better result in matters of longevity, wealth and strength than idols made of metal or stone.

The wooden idols indicate tribal origin of Jagannath worship among other things. When metal was unknown, the primitive people used to worship some trees as God. Probably, since the original idol of Nilamadhaba, worshipped by the tribal chief Biswabasu was a wooden one, the system continues. The crude wooden figures of Jagannath, etc., which are different from other Hindu gods, certainly give a tribal look. The aboriginal worship of the trees developed into worship of wooden figures. Even today the practice of the worship of the pole-shaped *Sthambeswari* is prevalent among the tribes and the tribal belt of Odisha. As a matter of fact, the tribal origin of Lord Jagannath is an admitted fact. The worship of the *gada*-shaped *Sudarshana* as a part of the *Chaturdha Murty* indicates its tribal origin. Similarly, during the time of *Anavashar*, the worship of the Lords is performed without the use of *tulasi* (basil leaf) and Ganga *jal* (water of the river Ganga); otherwise the two most important ingredients of the daily ritual. These two items are not used by the tribes in their worship. The *Daitapatis*, who exclusively perform the service of the idols from the *Snana Yatra* to the end of the *Ratha Yatra* (*Niladri Bije*), are considered as the descendants of the Sabara (Saora tribe) king Biswabasu, who was the original worshipper of Jagannath in the Nilamadhaba form in the Nilakandra inside the deep forest. According to legend, the deity Nilamadhaba, which happened to be the presiding deity of the Puri temple for quite some time before the establishment of the Triad, was originally being worshipped by the Sabara chief Biswabasu in the deep forest called Nila Kandara. No one other than Biswabasu had access to this secret place; not even his family members. Indradyumna, the King of Malawa (Puri), somehow came to know about Nilamadhaba and sent his Brahmin minister Bidyapati to locate the idol and to bring it to Puri. In spite of the fervent request of Bidyapati, the Sabara Chief, Biswabasu did not agree to show him the place of worship of Nilamadhaba as he also rightly feared that Bidyapati had a evil intention of stealing their God. Bidyapati cunningly succeeded in marrying Lalita,

8. *Paschima Dwara* of Sri Mandir.

7. Main Entrance, *Baisi Pahacha* with Patitapaban image.

the daughter of Biswabasu. Lalita somehow convinced her father that Bidyapati had no evil intention. Finally, Biswabasu, under pressure of his daughter, agreed to take Bidyapati to Nilakandara and show him the God in a blind-folded condition. But the clever Bidyapati succeeded in keeping a track of the route by secretly using mustard seeds all through the route. After the rainy season, when the mustard seeds germinated and grew up, the route became very clear for which finally Bidyapati was able to bring Nilamadhaba to Puri, by stealing it secretly.

The tribal origin of Jagannath is further emphasized by the existence of a group of *sevakas* known as *Daitas,* who are considered to be the descendants of Biswabasu. The *Daitas* are not Brahmin *sevakas*. But the descendants of Bidyapati and Lalita are known as Pati Mahapatras. They are Brahmin *sevakas*, engaged in different capacities in the Jagannath temple. Pati Mahapatra, the Brahmin *sevaka,* is the Head of the Daitapati *Niyoga,* the Association of the *Daita* and *Pati Mahapatra sevakas*. The *Daitas* and the *Pati Mahapatras* taken together are called *Daitapatis*. During the *Anavasara,* when they remain in total charge of the idols, the *Daitas* perform all activities except the offering of *Naivedya,* which is performed by the *Pati Mahapatra sevakas*. Even the *Daitas* will have to leave the place before the offering on orders from the *Pratihari sevakas*. However, the *Daitapatis* are considered as the relatives of Lord Jagannath, who perform all important *sevas* during the Nabakalebara ceremony including the observance of funeral obsequies for the death of the gods. The *Daitapatis* are specially entrusted with the services associated in close contact with the figures of the idols, such as dressing and moving them when they go out. However, the theory so far is restricted to legend only.

Besides this, traditionally it is also believed that the legendary King Indradyumna, who is supposed to have built the first temple at Puri and enshrined the gods inside, got the instruction in his dream that the idols are to be made out of the *Daru* that was floating in the sea. The *Rig Veda* also contains reference on the floating *Daru* in the sea out of which divine images were constructed. This partially explains the wooden origin of the images.

The presiding deities of the *Sri Mandira* are Jagannath, Balabhadra and Subhadra—the *Trimurty* (Trinity). With the inclusion of the *Sudarshana*, it becomes the *Chaturdha Murty*. Along with these four deities, three small idols of Bhu Devi (Biswa Dhatri), Sri Devi (Laxmi), and Nilamadhaba also adorn the *Ratna Bedi* (the pedestal on which the deities are seated) in the sanctum. The idol of Sri Devi, made of gold, is placed to the left and the idol of Bhu Devi, made of silver, is placed to the right of Lord Jagannath. The idol of Nilamadhab is made of wood (*Daru*) and is placed to the left of Lord Jagannath. In the Record of Rights of the Temple, Bhu Devi has been mentioned as Saraswati. Hence, along with the *Chaturdha Murty,* the Nilamadhaba is also made of *Daru*. All the seven idols taken together are called the *Saptamurty* or *Saptavarana*. Out of the seven idols, six are worshipped except that of

Nilamadhaba, which is not worshipped ostensibly for being identical or synonymous to Lord Jagannath. Nilamadahba, otherwise known as Madhab or Bala Purusottam, is considered as the *Kaa* or the representative deity (but not the *Chalanti Pratima*) of Lord Jagannath. It does not move out along with other deities during the *Snana Purnima* or the *Ratha Yatra*. As such, Nilamadhaba is believed to have been the original presiding deity of Puri temple, worshipped before the Trinity.

9. An ariel view of *Baisi Pahacha*.

When Does It Take Place?

It is normally believed that the Nabakalebara takes place during the *Mala Masa* or the *Joda Asadha* in every 12 years. It is pertinent to note that the Nabakalebara does not take place during every *Joda Asadha,* as normally the *Joda Asadhas* come more frequently than required. According to astronomical calculations, the *Joda Asadhas* sometimes come after 8, 11, 19 or 27 years. In the last one thousand years, during the existence of the temple, the *Joda Asadha* has come 72 times including that of 1996. Out of these 72 times, the 8th, 11th, 19th and 27th years have come 22, 16, 33, and 1 times, respectively.

As per the Hindu almanac, when one lunar month of *Asadha* is followed by another lunar month of *Asadha,* or in other words, when two lunar months of *Asadha* fall in one year, it is a fit case for the Nabakalebara. This second *Asadha* is an extra month, which is added to the lunar calendar after every 32 months and 16 days in order to make up the deficiency of a lunar month (29.5 days) with a solar month (30.44 days), i.e. 0.94 day of difference every month. Hence, after every 32 months and 16 days, one more lunar month of *Asadha* is added as a *Mala Masa* (month), otherwise known as *Purusottam Masa* or *Adhi*

Masa to bring a balance between the Solar year and the Lunar year. In other words, the Solar year has 365 days and 6 hours whereas the Lunar year has 354 days. Hence, there is a difference of 11 days and 6 hours between the Solar year and the Lunar year. This difference accumulates to one month in every 32 months and 16 days. However, this calculation is not always correct because the *Mala Masa* sometimes comes between 28th and 34th months. The year in which the *Joda Asadha* falls the extra month is intercalated after the first fortnight of the regular *Asadha* (*Suddha Asadha*) and ends before the last fortnight. In other words, the *Adhika Asadha* month is intercalated between the two fortnights of the *Suddha Asadha*. The *Sukla Pakhya* (bright fortnight) since the *Pratipada* after *Jyestha Purnima* up to the next *Amabasya* and the *Krushna Pakhya* of the second *Asadha* taken together constitute the *Suddha Asadha*. The middle period of one month between the two *Amabasyas* is *Purusottam Masa*. Hence, the first 15 days and the last 15 days of the two *Asadhas* constitute the *Suddha Asadha* and the middle month as the *Mala Masa* or *Adhika Asadha*.

According to the Record of Rights of the temple, the Nabakalebara takes place during the intercalary *Asadha*. Every year, after the *Snana Purnima,* the Lords necessarily become sick probably due to the ritualistic pouring of water during the ceremonial *snana* (bathing). During this period, the sanctum is closed for a fortnight for the secret *Anavasara Niti*. This period is utilized to make necessary repair and repainting of the idols among other things. The deities are not entirely made of wood. The wood constitutes the basic structure on which different layers of raisin, sandalwood paste and cloth pieces are wrapped. Every year, during the *Anavashara*, some wrappings are opened and new coatings are added. While doing this, the *Daitapatis* inspect if any damage has been caused to the wooden structure. If they come across signs of decay in the wooden structure, then they report the matter to the temple administration. *Khuri Nayak*, the temple astrologer and astronomer, and some other Pundits in turn take the appropriate decision as per scriptures to have the Nabakalebara ceremony during the next *Mala Masa*. As a matter of fact, the Nabakalebara or the total replacement of the idols, whenever necessary can only take place during the *Mala Masa*, which gives enough time for the preparation and consecration of the new idols with 45 days of *Maha Anavasara* as compared to the usual 15 days of *Anavashara* every year.

10. *Neelachakra* with *Patitapabana Bana.*

11. The *Patitapaban Bana* being tied by the *sevakas* (220 ft height).

There are two types of Nabakalaberas, i.e. the *Sriangaphita* (opening of the Holy Body) and the complete change of the idols as well as the transfer of *Brahma Pinda*. If the damage is less, then it is managed with only *Sriangaphita* during which the *Sri Anga* (Holy Body) of the deities are partially opened and the required repair work is done in the form of applying some new coatings of cloth, *chandan* (sandal paste), etc. During the *Sriangaphita,* the *Brahma Pinda* is not touched. If it is felt that the wooden portion has been damaged, or if the damage is beyond repair, then a total change of idols is recommended. Therefore, this decision to hold the Nabakalebara during the next *Mala Masa* is taken much before, i.e. before few years. Besides the condition of the idols, some other factors like the involvement of huge cost and elaborate ritualistic paraphernalia often makes it much more difficult to conduct it frequently. There have been instances in the past when the rulers of

Puri have not given their consent to conduct the Nabakalebara and have managed with only *Sriangaphita*. During the reign of the queen Suryamani Pata Mahadei, the Nabakalebara was avoided with only *Sriangaphita* because of the involvement of huge cost. In any case, such instances are rare.

The History of the Nabakalebara

The Nabakalebara is not an annual phenomenon of Jagannath like *Ratha Yatra*, *Snana Yatra* and *Chandana Yatra*. It is performed on periodical basis at regular intervals. In the absence of any recorded evidence, it is difficult to determine its exact period of commencement in the Jagannath Temple of Puri.

According to *Madala Panji*, after AD 1575, the Nabakalebaras have been held during 1593, 1608, 1625, 1646, 1665, 1684, 1698, 1714, 1730, 1749, 1768, 1790, 1809, 1828, 1836, 1855, 1874, 1893, 1912, 1931, 1950, 1969, 1977 and 1996. However, according to some authorities, so far Nabakalebara has been held 35 times and the 36th is due to be held in 2015.

The description of Nabakalebara is not found in the scriptures, which describe all the normal festivals of Jagannath. The Purusottam Mahatmya of *Skanda Purana*, written around AD 1300, describes almost all the festivals of Lord Jagannath but does not mention the Nabakalebara. It is believed that Nabakalebara is a later inclusion, which has emerged as a by-product of historical events wherein the reconstruction of the idols have become necessary due to the damages inflicted by the iconoclasts to the idols. The frequent invasion of Odisha in general and the Jagannath temple in particular for various reasons during the medieval period caused heavy damage to the temple as well as the gods, inside. Hence, the repair and replacement of the idols almost became a logical necessity in due course.

The earliest reference to the organization of Nabakalebara, according to the *Madala Panji,* is by Yajati Kesari II of Somavamsi dynasty in the 10th century AD (Yajati II ascended the throne sometime around AD 950). He originally belonged to Sambalpur-Sonepur region. After his occupation of the central Odisha, he somehow came to know that the idols of Lord Jagannath, Balabhadra and Subhadra of Puri have been buried under the ground at Sonepur. This has historical reference. Because of the invasion of Rakta Bahu on Puri from the side of the sea, the images were carried to a far-off place and buried under the ground at

12. The idols on the *Snana Mandapa*.

Sonepur, in order to save them from the invading iconoclasts. Yajati Kesari excavated the idols, after about 146 years, during which they had completely decayed and fallen into pieces. Hence, he made arrangement for the reconstruction of the idols as per the prescribed procedure and their reinstallation at Puri. This is therefore considered as the first recorded Nabakalebara.

Similarly, in 1568, Kalapahada, the General of the Sultan of Bengal, Suleiman Karrani annexed Odisha in general and Puri in particular. He carried the idols of Lord Jagannath and others to Bengal and burnt them on the banks of the River Hoogly. According to *Madala Panji,* one Bisara Mohanty somehow recovered the *Brahma Pinda* and with great care carried them in the trunk of a *mrudanga* (a musical instrument of *pakhawas* type) to Kujanga, where it was worshipped secretly till 1586. Ramachandra Deva I, the Raja of Khurdha, somehow came to know of it and made arrangement to bring it from Kujanga in 1586 and install in his own palace at Khurdha. Four years later, in 1590, he reinstalled it in the Jagannath temple at Puri. The idols reinstalled at Puri in 1590 therefore, contained the Brahma Pindas of the original idols. Therefore in the *Madala Panji,* Ramachandra Deva I has been described as the second Indradyumna, the holy ruler who constructed the temple and consecrated the God, inside. It is believed that since then the Nabakalebara has become a regular phenomenon.

The Jagannath temple has been attacked by invaders for about 18 times. The priests have taken the idols out of the temple 15 times in order to save them from being destroyed by the invaders. It is certain that the removal of the deities from the sanctum, the transportation, the concealment must have caused physical damage to the idols. As a matter of fact, more often the images have been buried under the ground or kept in makeshift houses, which must have caused serious damage to the wooden idols necessitating total or partial Nabakalebara from time to time. This period of political instability that made Nabakalebara a logical necessity gradually became a regular feature as a psychological measure to combat any future sacrilege. The continuity of the *Brahma Pinda* or the Life Substance was enough to retain the divinity of Jagannath not the physical aspects. In a way, the transitory and perishable nature strengthened the belief of the people in the humanistic character of the God.

Hence, logically it can be said with some amount of accuracy that the Nabakalebara of Lord Jagannath has become necessary because of foreign invasion. During the medieval period, such invasions became so frequent that the Nabakalebara almost became a regular affair making it a part of the system at least since 1590.

Sources on Nabakalebara

The authorities that describe different rituals of the Jagannath temple of Puri normally maintain silence on Nabakalebara. The Utkal Khanda of *Skanda Purana* written sometime during AD 1300 gives the details of the rituals of different festivals but remains silent on Nabakalebara. The

Utkal Khanda, however, contains elaborate description on the method of construction of the divine images but has no reference to the Nabakalebara. Similarly, the *Padma Purana*, *Brahma Purana*, *Naradiya Purana*, *Kapila Samhita*, *Bamadeva Samhita*, etc., which describe the rituals of the temple, also maintain stoic silence on Nabakalebara. Interestingly, the *Niladri Mohadaya* that is generally considered as the base source on all the rituals of the temple in general and that of the Nabakalebara in particular in reality does not contain any description on Nabakalebara at all. In any case, the rituals described in different sources are mostly annual in nature that reoccur every year but the Nabakalebara is neither an annual festival nor its occurrence can be predicted as it varies from 8 to 19 years depending on various conditions. But the same sources, however, have described the *Nitis* associated with the Solar or Lunar eclipses, which are not annual events as well.

The unrecognized *Indranilamani Purana*, which gives the description of Nabakalebara, is yet to be published in its regular form. Even the Record of Rights, which officially gives the details of different fairs and festivals, describes Nabakalebara in one small paragraph. This is because almost all the rituals associated with the Nabakalebara are *Gupta Nitis* (secret *seva*). Hence, the Nabakalebara and the associated rituals are mostly based on two sources. The first source is an unwritten tradition handed over from generation to generation of the *Sevayats* as a closely guarded secret. The second could be the numerous unpublished palm leaf manuscripts kept at the personal disposal of the *Daitas* and the *Pati Mahapatra* families to which no one else has any access. Whatever may be the authority or the source, the rituals are very rigid, time-bound and scrupulously followed without any scope for deviation. Any deviation may grievously injure the sentiments of the millions and millions of devotees all over the world.

Various Steps in the Process of Nabakalebara

The rituals associated with Nabakalebara are extremely esoteric and mostly performed with utmost secrecy and devoutness. The following rituals are performed with all devoutness during the Nabakalebara:

1. Location of the appropriate *Daru*, cut it in to size and transport it to Puri.
    a) Commencement of the process for the ceremony/*Vanayaga*;
    b) *Vanayaga*, i.e. to proceed in search of the *Daru*;

c) Identification, purification and cutting of *Daru*;
d) Transportation of the *Daru* to Puri.

2. The carving of the idols out of the *Daru*.
3. The consecration of the new idols and the transfer of the *Brahma Pinda*.
4. The sacred burial of the old idols and the funeral rites associated with it.
5. Giving the new idols their final shape by means of the required coatings, *Naba Yaubana Darshana* and the *Netrotsava*.

The Requirement of *Daru*

'Brahma Daru Namami' and 'Brahma Daru Smarami' are the prayers for Lord Jagannath. The location of the appropriate tree precedes a well-defined ritualistic procedure. The idols are carved out of the *Neem* (*Azadirachta indica*) tree. There is no explanation as to why the soft wood of *Neem* was selected for the purpose when other suitable trees like *Saal* (*Shorea robusta*), *Piasaal* (*Pterocarpus marsupium*), *Aswastha* (*Ficus religiosa*) and a host of other recommended trees are available in the Odishan forests in plenty. Probably because of its pungent juice and bitter taste, the *Neem* tree is less susceptible to natural decay and relatively free from attack by termites as compared to other trees. *Neem* also has great medicinal value. The *Vaikhanasa Agama* by Marichi does not mention *Neem* in the list of trees as being suitable for making of divine images. Normally, for making of divine images, the wood of *Aswastha, Saal, Piasaal, Saguan* (*Tectona grandis*), *Kendu* (*Diospyros marsupium*), *Khaira* (*Acacia catechu*), *Debadaru* (*Polilathia longifolia*), *Gambhari* (*Gmelina arborea*), etc. are used, all of which are available in the Odishan forests in plenty. Varahamihira, however, mentions *Neem* in the list of trees out of which divine images could be made. *Bamadeva Samhita* and the *Bhavisya Purana* also describe *Neem* as being suitable for the making of divine images, which can be worshipped by people of all castes (*Sarbabarnanga*). The *Daru* from which the divine idols are to be made must have some specific signs, which are specific to each deity.

Requirement of *Daru* for Lord Jagannath

The tree from which the idol of Lord Jagannath is to be made has to have the following features:

1. The colour of the tree should be dark as Lord Jagannath is dark in complexion.
2. The tree must have grown straight up to 12 feet with four principal branches symbolizing the four hands of Vishnu.
3. A water body like a river or a large pond must be nearby.
4. A cremation ground must be nearby.
5. An anthill must be close to the tree.
6. The tree must be without any bird nest.
7. No branch of the tree must have been cut.

13. The *chakra* (wheel) symbol on the tree trunk.

8. The tree must be located near a three-way or surrounded by three mountains.
9. No creepers must have grown on the tree.
10. *Varuna* (*Crateva magna*), *Sahada* (*Strebulus asper*) and *Billow* (*Aegle marmelos*) trees must be there close by.
11. A hermitage and a Shiva temple must be there, nearby.
12. There should be a few snake holes at the root of the tree or at least a few snakes must be creeping around the tree.
13. The tree must not have been struck by any lightning or its branches partially broken in the storm.
14. It should be away from the human settlement but should not stand on a swamp surrounded by marsh or mud.
15. On the trunk of the tree there must be natural impression of *shankha* (conch shell) and *chakra* (wheel).

It is generally accepted that the tree that contains at least five important signs of the above will be

14. The *shankha* (conch shell) symbol on the tree trunk.

15. *Padma* (lotus flower) symbol on the tree trunk.

considered suitable for the construction of the idol of Lord Jagannath.

Requirement of *Daru* for Balabhadra

1. The tree should be white or light brown in colour as Balabhadra is fair-complexioned.
2. The tree should have seven branches.
3. The upper branches and the twigs of the tree should give the look of a canopy or the hood of a cobra.
4. The tree should bear the symbol of a plough, the weapon of Balabhadra.

Requirement of *Daru* for Subhadra

1. The tree should have yellowish tinge.
2. It should have five branches.
3. The tree should bear the symbol of a lotus flower with five petals.

Requirement of the *Daru* for *Sudarshana*

1. The tree should have a reddish tinge.
2. The tree should have three branches.
3. There should be the sign of a *chakra* on the trunk.

Normally, great care is taken in finding a suitable tree with at least the minimum required signs for Jagannath. In case of other deities, simply the colour of the tree as required as per the colour of the idol and the sign symbolizing the respective weapons are looked for.

Different authorities have given different requirements for different idols, which though, by and large agree on important aspects yet differ on a number of points. Since there is no standard text or clear guideline to determine all these things, the tradition, experience and knowledge of the *Daitas* always matter. In any case it is strongly believed that they have some unpublished palm leaf manuscripts at their disposal to which others don't have access and everything is done according to that.

It is interesting to note that there is a great deal of difference between the old and established texts like the *Brihat Samhita* of Varahamihara and the tradition that is normally followed in Jagannath temple in matters of selection of wood. Varahamihara states that the tree to be chosen for the construction of divine images should not be ill formed, should not have been smitten by lightning or partially broken by storm, should not have been cut previously for any purpose, not destroyed by the elephants, must be free of bee hives and should not have fallen on the ground or dried up by itself. Though he does not specifically refer to Lord Jagannath, yet it is by and large applicable to all divine idols made of wood.

16. A tree with the required number of branches.

Some important aspects which are strictly forbidden by Varahamihara are traditionally treated as essential requirements in case of Jagannath. Varahamihara states that the trees that stand in a cremation ground, around a temple, near an ant hill, a penance grove, at the confluence of rivers and the ones which have been nurtured by human hands by bringing water in the pitchers, must be avoided for the purpose of the construction of divine images.

Similarly, Marichi in his *Vaikhyanasa Agama* also states that the trees that exist near an ant hill, which has serpents living at the roots, which stands near a cremation ground or a settlement of *chandals*, which is laden with flowers or fruits, which has birds living in it, which has been gnawed by the worms and which has been partially destroyed by fire or storm must be avoided for the carving of the divine images.

It is interesting to note that some of the features that have been forbidden by Varahamihara and Marichi, however, are being considered as important requirements for the *Daru* of Lord Jagannath.

Further, no distinction has been made regarding the gender of the trees. The trees also have the genders like feminine, masculine and neuter gender. It is stated that the tree that has a thick lower and slender upper is a *stri brukhya* (feminine tree), a tree with a thick or wide upper and slender lower is a *purusa brukhya* (masculine tree) and tree having the same girth throughout is a *nampusaka brukhya* (neuter tree). In the making of images for gods, masculine trees and for the making of images for goddesses, feminine trees should be used. In case of Jagannath and other images, this consideration of gender has not been taken into account though the *Neem* tree as such is a masculine tree.

The Order of Locating the *Daru*

The following order is maintained in locating the *Daru*. The same order is also followed in transporting the *Daru* to the temple as well as for the transfer of the *Brahma Pinda* in due course:

1. *Sudarshana*
2. Balabhadra
3. Subhadra
4. Jagannath

The *Vanayaga*

The journey for the search of the holy trees for the construction of the idols is called *Vanayaga* or trip to the forest to locate the *Daru*. The location of the sacred trees that fulfill the conditions requires nothing less than divine intervention. The process for the search of the tree begins by seeking the blessings of Lord Jagannath, 65 days before the *Snana Purnima* (*Jyestha Purnima*). All the four *Darus* must reach the temple before the *Snana Purnima*, the day on which the *Darus* are also given a ceremonial bath. After that the old images almost lose their idol status. Nevertheless, they are taken to the *Anavasara Pindi* but otherwise the waiting is for the new images to reach the sanctum.

The process for the search of the *Daru* begins from the *Chaitra Sukla Dasami* (the 10th day of the bright fortnight of the month of *Chaitra*). On this day, after the mid-day offering at an auspicious moment, the Pati Mahapatra goes up the *Ratna Bedi*, performs some *puja* and then takes out the specially made garlands from the person of all the four deities. These garlands, called the *Agnyamala* (the garlands of authorization), are handed over by the Pati Mahapatra to the leaders of the respective search parties, the *Daitas* called *Bada Daita*. The *Bada Bada Daita* (with the title of Das Mohapatra) receives the *Agnyamala* for Balabhadra, the *Majhi Bada Daita* (with the title of Das Mahapatra) receives for Subhadra and the *Mahaprabhunka Bada* (with the title of Swain Mahapatra) receives for Jagannath, respectively.

The *Agnyamala* of *Sudarshana* is retained by the Pati Mahapatra for himself. The word *Bada* in the temple terminology refers to the idols themselves. The *Agnyamalas* are carried as a mark of the Lords' command throughout the journey by the concerned persons till the respective sacred tree is located.

Thereafter, inside the *Anavasara Pindi* (between the Kalahat Dwara and the first wooden pole), the Bhitaraccha Mahapatra (the store keeper of the temple) ties the 12-*hata* (cubit) long *Khandua Pata* (*Baralagi Khandua Pata*) on the heads of the three *Badagrahi Daitas* and the Pati Mahapatra, the carrier of the *Agnyamalas*. The rest of the *Daitas* are presented with 4-*hata* long *Khandua Pata*. Then, at the *Jaya Vijaya Dwara,* the Bhitarchu Mahapatra binds full-length sarees on the forehead of the *Deula Karana* (temple accountant), *Tadhau Karana* (person in charge of the *Nitis* or rites of the Temple) and *Beharan Khuntia* (person in charge of the idols). Then the *Padhia Karan*, the *Lenka* and the *Maharanas* (Viswakarmas) are presented with cotton sarees. The *Deula Karana*, *Tadhau Karana* and the *Beharan Khuntia* are important functionaries associated with the process of Nabakalebara ceremony like the *Daitas* and the Pati Mahapatra, for which they are presented with silk sarees. This is called the *Saree Bandhana Niti*. Then the *Mekap* applies the sandal paste and vermilion paste on the forehead of all the members of the party after which they leave the temple through the Anand Bazar, Baishi Pahacha and the Simha Dwara. Thus begins the holy *Vanayaga Yatra* or the trip in search of the holy *Daru*. Simultaneously, the Brahmins make preparation in the Koili Baikuntha for the *Yagnasala*, the *Nirman Mandapa* and other *mandapas*.

The *Agnyamala* system is an important aspect of the temple, which denotes the order/authorization of the Lord to perform some specific responsibility. This is carried by the persons concerned till the tree is located. When the tree is located, the concerned garland (*Agnyamala*) is placed on the trunk of the tree.

Similarly, the sarees are presented to the authorized persons as authority to perform some specific responsibility on the orders of the Gajapati Maharaj, the *Adya Sevak* (first *sevak*) of the Lord. The presentation of a saree authorizes someone to perform some *seva* for the Lord, even if he is not a regular *sevaka*.

This holy robe of the Lord, worn as a turban by all the members of the party, and the carrying of the *Agnyamala* signifies that the Lord himself is travelling with the party. As such, Lord Jagannath is famous for such trips outside the temple to help the devotees and to protect the dignity of the kingdom. The famous Kanchi Kaveri episode, where Jagannath and Balabhadra proceeded on white and black horses respectively to Kanchi to help the Gajapati Purusottam Dev in the battle-field is a popular tradition.

There is no fixed principle as to how many people will take part in the *Yatra*. However, the categories of people or the *sevakas* who will take part in the *Yatra* is well defined. Normally, the following *sevakas* participate in the *Yatra* in different numbers from different categories, from time to time:

1. Rajaguru
2. Brahma
3. Brahmins
4. Pati Mahapatra
5. Deula Karana
6. Tadhau Karana
7. Daitas
8. Biswakarma Maharanas
9. Lenka
10. Barakandajas or temple police
11. General police personnel
12. Health, administrative and other officials

The Sevakas participating in the Vanayaga party in the recent past

Year	Raja Guru	Brahmana Purohita	Deula Karana	Pati Mohapatra	Daita	Lenka	Biswakarma Moharana	Barkandajas and others	Total
1950	1	5	1	1	19	1	4	18	50
1969	1	5	1	1	28	1	4	5	46
1977	1	4	1	1	32	1	4	4	48
1996	1	7	1+1 (Tadhau Karana)	1	47	1	4	4	67

One *Daita* belonging to a particular family is nominated as Biswabasu and the Pati Mahapatra as Bidyapati. The *Daitapati Niyoga* nominates them. As leaders of the party they take all important decisions relating to the trip. Almost all the *Daitapati* families are represented in the trip.

In the event of some untoward socio-religious incident happening before the commencement of the journey involving any member of the party like birth or death in the family, the concerned member is not dropped; rather, the *Yatra* is deferred to another suitable date.

After the commencement of the trip, no member can go back home on any pretext. If somebody falls sick on the way then he comes back and rests at Jagannath Ballava Matha till the entire team returns back to Puri with the *Daru*. In spite of so many hazards and strenuous efforts associated with the *Yatra*, no untoward incident has ever happened in the recent past.

The Commencement of the *Yatra*

After leaving the temple amidst beating of drums, trumpets and gongs, blowing of conch shells and the accompaniment of *samkirtan* (singing of religious songs, accompanied by music and dance), the party proceeds on the Bada Danda (Grand Road) to the Royal Palace to seek the blessings of the Gajapati Maharaja for the success of the mission. The Gajapati Maharaja personally comes out, meets the search party and gives his blessings by presenting betel nuts, coconuts, *tandula* (sanctified rice) and other auspicious articles including some pieces of gold in two metallic plates to the Rajaguru. One of the plates is handed over by the Rajaguru to *Biswabasu* or Bidyapati (Patimahapatra), the leaders of the party, and the other is retained by himself as the representative of the Brahmins. This is called the *Guateka Niti*. After obtaining the royal permission, the party proceeds towards the

17. The *Agnyamala* being held by the *Bada Daitas*.

18. The *Guateka Niti – Vanayaga*, 1996.

Jagannath Ballava Matha, which is associated with many holy saints like Ray Ramananda and Sri Chaitanya, where it halts for one-and-a-half day to make final preparation for the trip as well as the logistics. Then they proceed to Kakatapur, about 50 km from Puri via Ramchandi and Konark. At Kakatpur, the party halts at Deuli Matha on the bank of the holy river Prachi on the outskirts of Kakatapur. Tradition holds it that the place was the original seat of Goddess Mangala, which was later shifted to the present site after the construction of the temple. Messengers are sent to the temple of Goddess Mangala to announce the arrival of the party. On receiving the news (*chitau*) of the arrival of the party at the Deuli Matha, the priests of the temple make proper arrangement to receive the party and proceed in a grand procession along with *ghanta* (gong), *mardala* and other instruments to welcome the party. Then the party enters the temple with full religious honour as the representative of Lord Jagannath to Goddess Mangala. After performing the required worship in the temple, the party returns back to the Matha, where they halt for the total period of their stay at Kakatapur. During this

Top:
19. The Gajapati Maharaja, Dibyasing Dev in the midst of the members of the party.

Bottom:
20. View of Sri Nahar—Gajapati with the party.

period the red flag (Neta) of Lord Jagannath, brought from Puri, is tied at the *shikhara* (top) of the Mangala Temple.

21. Divyasing Dev, present Gajapati Maharaj.

22. The Deula Karan, Rajaguru and other members of the party in front of the Sree Nahara.

The Deuli Matha or Siddha Deuli Matha is under the direct control of the famous Emar Matha of Puri. During the Nabakalebara of 1977, the Deuli Matha was in a dilapidated condition for which the party was accommodated at the nearby Someswar Siva temple but the paraphernalia of receiving the team at the Matha and the return of the party to the Matha was fully observed; only that some members of the party preferred to stay at the Someswar temple. In any case, the custom of halting at the Matha is not very old. The Matha is very small but has a spacious garden where the members of the party sleep under the tree. Probably the system of halting at the Matha started since 1912. Earlier, the entire team used to stay inside the Mangala Temple itself.

The journey up to Kakatapur is covered on foot. Their personal belongings, other provisions as well as the religious requirements are placed on bullock carts. The leaders of the party, *Bidyapati* and the *Biswabasu*, if they feel like, can sit in the bullock cart or otherwise all others cover the entire distance on foot and quite naturally without shoes.

The Lenka Sevaka leads the party holding the silver *Sudarshana Chakra* in his hands. It normally takes two days to reach Kakatapur. On the way, wherever necessary, the team halts for the night. The *Daitas* of the party are not supposed to rest under someone else's roof. Hence, they take rest under the tree and cook their own food (*habisharna*). The Brahmins, however, are not bound by this rule and can rest in a temple or a school or a *matha*. During the period of their stay at Kakatapur, the team lives on the *prasad* of Goddess Mangala, though sometimes the *Mahaprasad* is brought from Puri.

23. The Jagannath Ballava Matha where the *Vanayaga* party rests for the logistics.

24. The members of the party resting inside the Jagannath Ballava Matha.

25. The members of the party resting inside the Jagannath Ballava Matha.

26. The bullock carts carry the provision for the party.

Mangala of Kakatapur and the Dream

Kakatapur is the seat of Goddess Mangala, who gives direction to the party to locate the trees. At Kakatpur, the team rests for several days. When all the members of the party stay at Deuli Matha, the Acharya, the Brahmins and the Pati Mahapatra remain in the temple and sleep inside the temple.

27. The Deuli Matha, Kakatpur.

28. The Deuli Matha, Kakatpur.

29. The Deuli Matha.

Top right:
30. Jagannath being worshipped at Deuli Matha.

Bottom right:
31. Balabhadra being worshipped at Deuli Matha.

During this period, either the Pati Mahapatra or the Acharya is supposed to get the direction of the location of the trees in his dream from the Goddess Mangala. Normally, they wait for 3 days and mutter the *Swapnavati Mantra* for 108 times

Top:
32. The *chitau* (notification), being written by Chandan Hajuri, the *Deula Karan* at Deuli Matha.

Bottom:
34. The party rests at Deuli Matha.

Top:
33. The *Agnyamalas* at the resting place.

Bottom:
35. The party rests at Someswar Temple.

before going to bed to have the dream. After 3 days, if no instruction is received, then extensive worship of Goddess Mangala takes place when her entire body is covered with flowers. The first flower falling down from the idol is taken as the direction in which the first tree could be found and the following three flowers for the following three trees as per the order indicated earlier. The trees for four different gods are invariably located at four different places. For all these days, the *Daitas* go out in search of suitable trees in different directions and come back in the evening. They are divided in two to three teams as per the decision of the leaders of the party and proceed in different directions in search of the tree. Sometimes, the people on their own inform the team about the

36. The procession from Deuli Matha towards Mangala Temple.

37. Goddess Mangala, Kakatpur.

existence of the tree as the required signs are well-known. In any case, identification of suitable trees has never been a problem so far.

It seems that the idea of involving Goddess Mangala is of later origin. Originally, the team used to go to Kakatapur in search of the trees as the Prachi valley continues to have a deep forest with plenty of *Neem* trees. Initially, the team might be taking rest or halting in the temple but the ritualistic involvement of the Goddess Mangala seems to be a later addition. In this connection, it is important to note that when Bimala is the presiding deity of Puri, why does the party go up to Kakatapur to seek the blessings of Goddess Mangala? Mangala, besides being the most important of the eight *Shaktis* (*Asta Shakti*) who are protecting the Purusottam Khetra, is associated with the Prachi valley, which has a deep forest around. According to the Utkal Khanda of *Skanda Purana*, the *Astha Shakti* associated with the protection of Purusottam Khetra are Mangala, Bimala, Sarba Mangala, Ardhasani, Alamba, Kalaratri, Marichika and Chandika.

Top:
38. The main entrance of Mangala Temple.

Bottom:
39. Side view of Mangala Temple.

In any case, as the process goes, the trees are found independent of the Goddess. According to the *Shastras,* the *Darus* are to be brought either from the east or the north or the intermediate direction of north-east, i.e. *aishnya kona*, which also suits Kakatapur.

Though traditionally Goddess Mangala is supposed to give the direction for the location of the trees, yet it is believed that the surreptitious, esoteric and unpublished palm leaf manuscripts, at the disposal of the *Daitapatis*, which contain elaborate description of the Nabakalebara, also contains the names of the places where the four trees will be found hundreds of years before. It is a fact that Prachi Valley used to have a dense forest of *Neem* trees. Hence, in the past probably almost all the trees were available in the Prachi Valley itself. With the passage of time, people have become aware of the required signs for the trees. And that is how availability is being reported from far-off places.

The *Vanayaga* Ceremony

After one respective *Daru* is identified, the *Biswakarma* gives the final approval of the

Top:
40. Inner view of Mangala Temple.

Bottom:
41. Inside of Mangala Temple.

42. The three *Agnyamalas* and the *Sudarshana*.

suitability of the particular tree after necessary measurement and verification of different aspects from different angles. Then a coconut is offered as a mark of finality of selection. The *Sudarshana Chakra* brought by the *Lenka* from the temple is put near the root of the tree to ward off evil spirits. Once a tree is identified, all the members of the team reach the spot and start the *yagna* and other associated activities one after the other in the same order as *Sudarshana*, Balabhadra, Subhadra and Jagannath. After purification of the tree and the surroundings the *Agnyamala* of the concerned deity, brought by the *Bada Daita* or the *Pati Mahapatra* as the case may be, is placed on the tree to establish a link between the concerned deity and the tree. It is important that all the members of the team proceed to all the trees for the *Vanayaga* ceremony.

43. The *Deula Karan* with Jagannath Swain Mohapatra (L) the *Bada Daita* for Jagannath.

44. *Lenka Sevaka* with the *Sudarshana*.

Then the *yagnasala* (sacrificial pavilion) is constructed to the western side of the tree with specific length and breadth, and four gateways (*toranas*) and thatched roof. The *Ankuraropan* (sowing of some specific types of seeds for germination) is performed and a full-scale *yagna* takes place generally for three days. During this period, the Acharya, the Brahmins, the *Pati Mahapatra* and the *Daitapatis* live inside the *Yagnasala*, and other members of the party live in the temporary huts called the *Sabara Palli*, constructed for the purpose. The *Sabara Palli* is constructed in the line of tribal houses, covered with leaves and branches of the trees.

After the completion of the *yagna*, the tree is worshipped with the mantra of the concerned deity, whose idol is going to be carved out of its *Daru*. Then it is smeared with the *vasma* of the *yagna*, bathed in holy water, ghee and other things and wrapped in white cloth and a *pani kakharu* (pumpkin) is sacrificed with all rituals. The gold, silver and iron axes laying in the *yagnasala* are worshipped and charged with the *Sudarshana Mantra*. Next, the *Acharya* would offer the golden

Top:
45. The *Sudarshana* is placed on the tree.

Bottom:
46. The concerned *Agnyamala* placed on the tree.

axe to the *Pati Mahapatra* (*Bidyapati*) to begin the sacred cutting. *Pati Mahapatra* goes round the tree clockwise and gives a few symbolic strokes to cut the tree and takes the golden axe as his due for the service. The Acharya then offers the silver axe to *Biswabasu,* who gives some symbolic strokes with the silver axe, which he also takes as his due for the service. Finally, the iron axe is handed over to the *Biswakarma Maharana,* who begins the process of the real cutting. It seems that the ceremonial cutting of the tree by *Bidyapati* and *Biswabasu* with golden and silver axes respectively is of later origin as the description of the same is not found in many sources. The tree should fall in the eastern, northern or north-eastern direction. Falling in any other direction is considered as inauspicious. Unlike the normal cutting of a tree, this cutting begins from the bottom and then it is cut into pieces as per the required measurement.

During the entire period, 108 names of the God Patala Nrusingha is chanted to make the process hassle-free. The entire party maintains strict austerity and takes *habisharna* and that too once a

Top:
47. Purification of the tree.

Bottom:
48. Jagannath Swain Mohapatra (R) with Rajkishore Das Mohapatra, the *Biswabasu* (L).

day. Normally, the whole process takes six to ten days at one tree.

Only the trunks of the trees called the *chaupata* are required for the preparation of the idols. A log of 96 *yabas* in length and 24 *yabas* in breadth on each side is cut off from the tree. The rest of the portion including the branches and the leaves is buried on the same spot under the ground. The *Daru* is debarked, given a quadrangular shape, wrapped in a silken cloth (*khandua patta*) and transported to Puri. While cutting the tree, necessary signs are given to identify the top and bottom sides for the convenience of the *Maharanas* at the time of the carving of the idols.

Sometimes the thick branches are not buried. These are reduced to small and convenient size and carried to Puri to be used for the arms of Lord

Facing page (No. 36):

Top left:
49. The *Biswabasu*, *Deula Karan* and the *Bada Daita*.

Top right:
50. *Yagna* near the tree.

Centre left:
51. *Yagna* near the tree.

Centre right:
52. *Yagna* near the tree.

Bottom left:
53. *Yagna* near the tree.

Bottom right:
54. *Barakandaj*, the temple police guarding the tree.

Top:
55. The sacred cutting.

Bottom:
56. The *Daru* is being debarked and cut to quadrangular shape.

Jagannath and Balabhadra, if necessary. It is kept in mind that the branches of the tree are used for that particular God for which they have been collected and not for any other God. In the event of not being required immediately, the branches are kept in store to meet the future repair of some part or finally given to the Mathas or other Jagannath temples for the construction of their images.

Find-spots of the respective *Darus* in the recent past

Year	*Sudarshana*	Balabhadra	Subhadra	Jagannath
1912	Fategada, Puri	Niali Hata, Cuttack	Udayapur, Puri	Prataprudrapur, Nuasahi
1931	Kakatapur, Puri	Satwikpur, Cuttack	Niali, Cuttack	Gabapada, Cuttack
1950	Jalaipur, Puri	Nuapatna, Banamalipur, Puri	Durgeswar, Nuahata, Puri	Khadihara, Jagatsinghpur, Cuttack
1969	Balara, Banamalipur, Puri	Gadacharipur, Balipatna, Puri	Kanhupur, Gobindapur, Cuttack	Champa jhara, Tapanga, Khurda
1977	Singha Sahi, Niali, Cuttack	Bhogeswar, Adashpur	Berboi, Delanga, Khurda	Hatasahi, Biswanathpur, Puri
1996	Bisoidiha, Niali, Cuttack	Rama Krushna pur, Salepur, Cuttack	Malada, Astaranga, Puri	Dadhimachhagadia, Khurda

Transportation of the *Daru*

During the cutting of the tree, the cart to carry the *Daru* to Puri is also prepared. The type of the cart, its length, breadth and the wood to be used for different parts follows a well-defined principle. The cart is 8 *hatas* (cubits) in length with two main *dandas* (main bars) and a few supporting planks as cross-bars. It is to have four solid wheels, without spokes, formed by joining of three planks bound together with the support of iron clamps. The *dandas* are made of *Tentuli* (*Tamarindus indica*) wood. The body is prepared out of *Kendu* (*Diospyros melanoxylon*) wood and the wheels are of *Bara* (*Ficus beghalensis*) wood. This practically explains the reason as to why the tree to be selected should not stand alone and must be surrounded by other trees.

The quadrangular-sized *Daru* is wrapped in coloured silken cloth and then lifted to the cart with loud chanting of necessary *mantra*. It is

57. Preparation of the cart for the transportation of the *Daru*.

firmly tied to the cart with ropes prepared out of cane to avoid the risk of falling down on the way. These days, when enough cane is not available, coconut ropes are also being used though the use of cane rope is a must even in small quantity, in a symbolic form. All through the route the cart is pulled by human hands and not by any other means. Thousands of devotees from the villages enroute pull the cart with great enthusiasm and devotion. The entire distance is covered by *samkirtan*, chanting of *mantras* and blowing of *ghanta, mardal, dhupa, deepa,* etc. The atmosphere throughout the journey becomes extremely pious. Thousands of people get involved in the entire process.

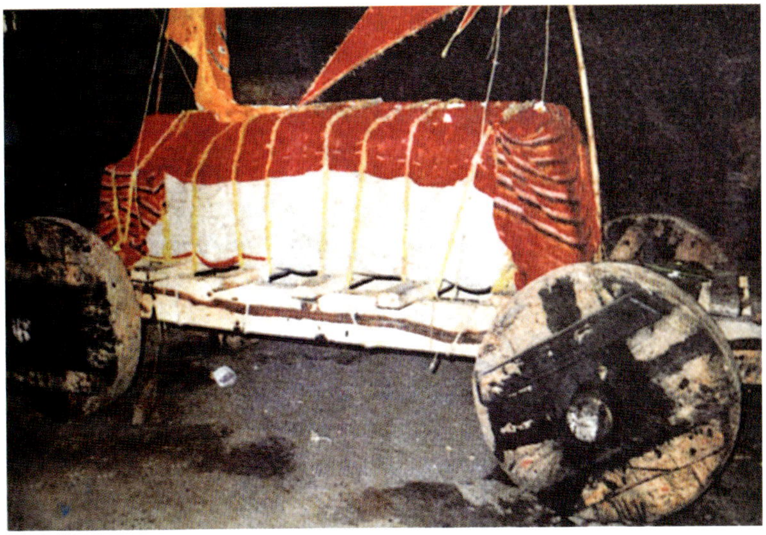

Top:
58. The *Daru* is covered with red silken cloth and loaded on the cart.

Bottom:
59. Transportation of the *Daru*.

If some untoward incident happens on the way or if the cart breaks down, then the party goes to the nearest Vishnu temple, and offers 108 *Nrusingha Mantra* after which necessary repair work is done and the journey resumes.

The order of transportation of the *Daru* is the same as described above for the location of the tree. Depending upon the location, if the *Daru* reaches Puri from the side of Sakhigopal on the National Highway, then it halts at the Alamchandi Temple near Atharanala. If the cart comes on the Marine Drive, then it halts at the Nrusingh temple near Gundicha temple. Ceremonial information is sent to the Gajapati Maharaja as well as to the temple administration about the arrival of the *Daru*. The temple authorities come out to receive the *Daru* with full religious honour. Sometimes the Gajapati Maharaja personally joins the procession, normally for the *Daru* of Lord Jagannath to add. The *Darus* are taken in a grand procession first to the *Simha Dwara* and then through the north gate (Elephant *Dwara*) up to the four temporary *Daru Gruhas* made for the purpose along the compound wall of *Koili Baikuntha*. The four *Darus* are kept in the respective *Daru Gruhas*

Top:
60. *Daru Sagadi* enroute.

Bottom:
61. *Daru* passing through a village.

Top:
62. Transportation of *Daru*, 1969.

Bottom:
63. *Daru* enroute, 1969.

Top right:
64. The Alam Chandi Temple.

Bottom Right:
65. The Nrusingha Temple.

along with the same *sagadas* (carts) in which these have been brought. The preparation for the sheds begins right from the commencement of the *Vanayaga*.

All the *Darus* must reach the temple before the *Snana Yatra*, the day on which these are also given the ceremonial bath, after which the process for the preparation of the new idols begins. Till the ceremonial bathing, the *Pati Mahapatra* worships the *Daru* daily in the *Daru Gruha*.

Preparation of the Idols

During *Snana Purnima,* for the sacred bath of the idols, 112 *gadus* (pitcher) of water is brought from the *Suna Kuan* (Golden Well) near the *Uttar Dwara* (North Gate) of the temple, which is added with *karpura* (camphor), *chandana* (sandal paste), *chua, keshara*, etc. before pouring them on the idols. Out of the 112 *gadus* of water, 4 *gadus* are set aside and taken to the temporary *Daru Gruha* in the Koili Baikuntha and the *Darus* are given a ceremonial bath with that sacred water. After this, the *Darus* become sacred and the old idols almost lose their sanctity. Nevertheless, they are taken to the *Anavasara Pindi* and await the arrival of new idols.

During the Nabakalebara, the *Anavasara* period extends to 45 days and is called the *Maha Anavasara* as against the usual period of 15 days. This period of 45 days is divided into three parts of 15 days each for different ceremonies.

1. The first two weeks, i.e. the dark fortnight of the *Suddha Asadha* is devoted towards the carving of the idols, the simultaneous holding of the consecration or *Daru Nyasa,* shifting of the new idols to the temple (*Anavasara Pindi)* the transfer of the *Brahma Pinda* from the old idols to the new idols and the sacred burial of the old idols.
2. During the second fortnight, i.e. the bright fortnight, which is the first fortnight of the extra/*Adhika Asadha,* the *Daitas* observe funeral rites and not much action is taken during the fortnight as regards the idols.
3. During the third part, i.e. the second fortnight (dark fortnight) of the extra/*Adhika Asadha,* the wooden images, considered as skeletal part, are added with flesh and blood by wrapping silken and cotton cloth and other items. After that, different colours are applied and finally the *Puja Panda* paints the pupils of the eyes.

In the first phase, the construction of the idols as well as the consecration of the *Daru* goes on simultaneously at *Koili Baikuntha* from the *Asadha Krushna Dwitia tithi* onwards. On the *Chaturdashi,* the *Nyasa Daru* as well as the wooden idols are moved to the temple one by one in ceremonial procession at midnight.

66. The three new stone bases at *Nirmana Mandapa*, *Bije chaki* (painting).

A total of seven *mandapas* are constructed inside the *Koili Baikuntha*, which are covered with temporary thatched roof. These are *Nrusingh Mandapa, Nirman Mandapa, Pratistha Mandapa, Daru Mandapa, Sambhara Mandapa, Snana Mandapa,* and *Adhibasa Mandapa*. The size, shape and the direction of all the *mandapas* follow a well-defined procedure. All the *mandapas* are to be completed two days before the *Snana Yatra*.

After the holy bathing of the *Daru* during the *Snana Purnima,* all the *Darus* are shifted from the

among a few other theories. Since then hearing of the sound of the construction is considered inauspicious for the persons who are not associated with the construction in any way. It is believed that if someone sees it, he becomes blind and if one hears the sound he becomes deaf. Hence, to avoid people from seeing or hearing the sound a continuous chanting of *Veda*, singing of *bhajanas*, the *samkirtan*, banging of *telingi baja* and drums, even the dancing of the *devadasi* (if available) go on outside the enclosure.

During the second stage, i.e. during the bright half of the extra *Asadha*, not much action is taken on the idols. The *Daitas* observe the funeral rites during this period for the loss of someone who has been so near and dear to them. The new idols remain standing in the *Anavasara Gruha* and as usual isolated and hidden from the public view behind the bamboo curtain, while the *Pati Dian*, i.e. the paintings on the bamboo curtain are worshipped. The moving deities or the *Chalanti Pratimas* of Madanmohana for Jagannath, Dolagobinda for Balabhadra, Lakshmi and Viswadhatri for Subhadra, Nrusingha and *Sudarshana* are worshipped during this period.

During the third stage, i.e. during the dark half of the *Adhika Asadha,* steps are taken to add flesh and blood to the wooden idols (*Saptabharana*) through thick coatings of different materials. Actually the work begins from the *Krushna Chartudashi* night. The carpenters prepare the wooden structures, which are considered as the skeletal forms (bones) of the idols. The flesh and blood part is applied later by the *Daitas* and the *Pati Mahapatra* to complete the idols.

The *Madala Panji* and the *Niladrimohadaya* give an elaborate description of the annual repair of the deities, which also applies to the new ones. The human body is made up of seven *dhatus* as bone, bone marrow, blood, vein and nerve, flesh, skin and the semen. The wooden structure, considered as the bone part of the idols, is applied with perfumed oil, prepared by mixing it with some specific flowers and by preserving it for quite some time to make it fragrant. This is considered as the bone marrow part. Red threads are wrapped all around on the entire structure for blood vessels. Stripes of cotton cloth, called *netapatta,* are also wrapped over the entire structure. A thick paste of camphor, musk, sandal paste, etc. is applied for flesh. This is expected to provide features or the contours of the figures. Then strong stripes of cotton cloth are wrapped for the skin. After that starch is applied as adhesive to strengthen all the coatings. This is known as *Saptavarana Karma*.

Large quantity of these materials is used including the silken cloth for the purpose. The process continues to be the same for centuries. No change or variation is permitted.

After the idols are given their final shape, the temple *chitrakaras*, known as the *Dutta Mahapatras,* paint the idols. This is called the *Banaka Lagi* or *Purna Sri Angaraga*. Since the *Daitapatis* have already completed the work up to the skin in the *Saptavarana Karma*, the work of the *chitrakaras* is considered as preparing the hair (*roma*) on different parts of the body. The painting is done with indigenous colour like charcoal for black, the powder of mothers of pearl for white and the turmeric for yellow, etc. They take two days (the 14th and the New Moon day) to finish the work.

After the *Banaka Lagi* or *Purna Sri Angaraga,* the *Nabayaubana Darshana* or the first public appearance (*darshana*) of the Lords takes place on the *Amavasya* day. The first *darshana* of the Lords on the *chaka pindi* (stone base) of the *Anavasara Gruha* is called the *Nabayaubana Darshana*. According to the Uktal Khanda of *Skanda Purana,* on this day, i.e. on the *Asadha Amabasya* day, the *Bidyapati*, the Brahmin minister of the legendary king Indradyumna had the occasion to have the first *darshana* of Nilamadhaba on the Nilakandara, while under the worship of the Savara king Biswabasu. Further, it was on this *Asadha Amabasya* day that the first *darshana* of the Lords was held while the idols were being constructed for the first time during the period of the legendary king Indradyumna.

The painters however don't paint the pupils of the eyes of the idols, which is considered as the finishing touch. On the *Pratipada* day, i.e. the first day of the bright half of the regular *Asadha*, the *Puja Panda*, the Brahmin priest paints the pupils of the eyes with great care and with full ceremonial rites. The *Dutta Mahapatras* offer black colour in three different silver pots (*bata*) with sticks to paint the pupils of the eyes. This is called as the *Netrostova*. After the *Netrostova*, the idols are given a symbolic purificatory bath. A bronze mirror is placed in front of them and their reflections are bathed in the mirror (*Bimba Snana*) with *Panchamruta* and other necessary things. Thus ends the Nabakalebara ceremony and the idols are ready for the *Ratha Yatra* on the next day, i.e. the *Dwitia* day.

The Idols

The measurement of the different parts of the idols is a closely guarded secret of the *Daitapatis*. Nothing is left to chance. All the parts have a definite shape and size, which must be scrupulously followed. Except *Madala Panji,* no other source gives any information in this regard. Such perfection cannot be based on imagination or tradition. Hence, there must be some unpublished palm leaf manuscripts or other records at the disposal of the *Daitapatis* to carry on the work with such perfection and precision. The *Madala Panji* however contains the following measurement of the idols. In any case, the measurement of different parts is a secret.

The height of Lord Jagannath is 84 *yabas*. The two outstretched arms taken together also measure 84 *yabas*. He is round-shaped and dark-coloured.

The height of Balabhadra is 84 *yabas* with arms of 73.5 *yabas*. He is conch shell-shaped and white complexioned.

The height of Subhadra is 52.5 *yabas*. She is lotus-shaped and yellow-coloured.

The *Sudarshana* is 84 *yabas* long, log-shaped (*gadakruti*) and red coloured.

For the convenience of the construction and to maintain perfect measurement, the height of each idol has been divided into 32 *bhagas*. In other words, one *bhaga* for Jagannath and Balabhadra comes to 2.625 *yabas* whereas for Subhadra it comes to 1.625 *yabas*, approximately.

A *yaba* is a local measurement, equivalent to the middle part of the middle finger of the carpenter doing the job. It is approximately 1 inch or 2.5 cm.

The length of the *Daru* of Jagannath as brought from the find-spot after cutting is 96 *yabas*. The idol of Jagannath iconographically consists of five parts, i.e. *srimukha* (face), *uraka* (neck), *hia* (heart), *paridhapana* (waist) and *sri payara* (feet). The measurement of the parts in *bhagas* is 14, 5, 3, 4 and 6, or in other words 36.75, 12, 9, 10.5 and 15.75 *yabas,* respectively.

The idol of Balabhadra consists of four parts as *phana* with *srimukha* (face), uraka (neck), *hia* (heart) with *paridhapana* (waist) and the *payara* (feet). The measurement as given in *bhagas* is 12, 4, 6 and 10 corresponding to 31.5 (the snake hood 6, fore head 1.5 and the face 24 *yabas*), 10.5, 15.75 and 26.25 *yabas,* respectively.

The arms of Jagannath and Balabhadra are carved separately and joined to the body. Each arm is made up of two separate logs, one inserted into the head and protruding towards the left or right and the other one joined to it projecting towards the front.

The length of both the arms of Jagannath taken together comes to 84 *yabas,* equivalent to His own height. Each arm has a length of 42 *yabas*. The side arms are of 20 *yabas,* out of which 12 *yabas* are invisible as these are inserted into the head. Hence, only 8 *yabas* of the side arms are visible. The arms projecting to the front are 22 *yabas* each. Thus, each arm is 42 *yabas,* out of which 12 *yabas* are not visible for being inserted into the head. The height and the arms being equal, i.e. 84 *yabas,* the idol of Jagannath is round-shaped (*chakrakruti*).

The arms of Balabhadra are of 36.75 *yabas* each or 73.5 *yabas* in toto. These are also divided into two parts. The side arms have a total length of 13.75 *yabas* each, out of which 7 *yabas* are inserted into the head for which only 6.75 *yabas* are visible as extending to each side. The length of the arms extending to the front are 23 *yabas* each, which makes it 1 *yaba* more than that of Jagannath though the total length of both the parts of the arm including the invisible portions comes to 73.5 for Balabhadra whereas for Jagannath it comes to 84 *yabas*. The idol of Balabhadra takes the shape of a conch shell, maybe because of longer front arms and slender legs.

Subhadra, iconographically, is divided into four parts, i.e. the *srimukha* (face), the *hia* (heart), *paridhapana* (waist) and the *payara* (feet), measuring 12, 2, 12 and 6 *bhagas,* respectively corresponding to 19.75, 3.25, 19.75 and 19.75 *yabas*. Subhadra is lotus-shaped and standing on a thin body. It is said that the arms of Subhadra are kept hidden inside the body.

The *Sudarshana* is of the same height as Jagannath and Balabhadra, i.e. 84 *yabas*. It also consists of four parts of 8 *bhagas* each. It is pole (*gada*) shaped. A real miniature gold discus weighing 16 *palas* is inserted into it, probably at the time of consecration.

The small idol of Madhaba or Nila Madhaba, identical or a small replica of Jagannath, made of wood is also prepared by the *Maharanas* along with other idols. Not much is known about its size, the *Daru,* out of which it is made or other details. Probably the *Brahma Pinda* of the Madhaba idol is also changed along with others and the work is performed by *Pati Mahapatra,* who does it for Jagannath. This thereby means many far-reaching things, which otherwise have not found mention in any important source. If this is accepted, then first of all the *Nyasa Daru* has to be cut into five pieces instead of four as mentioned in different sources. Secondly, it has to find a place in the order of entry of the idols into the temple and such other things. But whether mentioned or not, its existence is a matter of fact. Probably because of its close association with Jagannath, not much has been mentioned about it meaning thereby what is done for Jagannath is also done for Madhaba.

Consecration of the Images

Along with the progress of the work of construction of the idols in the *Nirmana Mandapa* by the carpenters, the work of the consecration of the idols by the priests goes on simultaneously at the *Pratistha Mandapa*. The length and breadth of the *Pratistha Mandapa* have to be either 16 x 16 or 12 x 12 *hatas*. In the middle of the *Mandapa,* a fire altar (*bedi)* of 5 *hatas* and 8 *angulis* is prepared for the *yagna*. There are three other *mandapas* around the *Pratistha Mandapa*, called the *Snana Mandapa*, *Adhibasa Mandapa* and the *Sambhara Mandapa*. The *Nyasa Daru* is consecrated (*Prana Pratistha*) here by the Brahmin Priests, the *Rajaguru*, the *Acharya* and some others. The *Gajapati Maharaja* or his representative nominates the *Acharya*, the Chief Priest, to perform the *Pratistha* ceremony, preferably from the *Rajaguru* family. He is assisted by a number of other Brahmins to complete the job. It is essential that the *Acharya* should be well-versed with the *Nrusingha Mantra*, which is considered as the main *mantra* for the consecration.

Unlike other gods and goddesses, the *Prana Pratistha* does not take place with the original idols itself. It is performed on a piece of wood, called *Nyasa Daru*, cut from any one of the four *Darus* (most probably from the *Daru* of Subhadra). It is not possible to consecrate the original idols because they are not ready by that time nor the process can wait till the idols are ready. Hence, the processes of the consecration as well as the preparation of the idols go on side by side and simultaneously because of a very rigid, time-bound schedule. The consecration ceremony goes on for two weeks. The consecration is done extensively in different stages as *Abhisheka, Nyasa* and *Yagna* (sacrifice). The Laxmi-Nrusingha image is worshipped for the entire duration. The movable metallic Laxmi-Nrusingha image brought from the small temple meant for all the movable idols near the *Mukti Mandapa* is placed to the south-east corner of the *Pratistha Mandapa* and worshipped by the *Pati Mahapatra* daily in the morning as the commencement of the day's worship. This movable Laxmi-Nrusingha image is used only during the Nabakalebara. The fire sacrifice begins from the 6th day of the commencement of the consecration ceremony. Here again the main God is Nrusingha and major part of the oblations is offered to him. Though some sort of *bali* (sacrifice) is offered to the *Dasa Digapalas* and the unknown spirits daily, yet on the Saptami day one live Magura fish (African catfish/*Clarias gariepinus*) is sacrificed, parts of which are buried outside the *yagnasala* in ten different directions i.e. the *Dasa Diga*. This is something uncommon in a Vaishnavite temple. The *Nyasa* is done separately for the three idols, though with the same piece of *Daru*, which is cut into four pieces later. Along the *Mantraraja-Nrusingha Nyasa* for all the three deities, the *Kesavadi-Nyasa* is performed for Lord Jagannath, the Saivite *Sri Kanthadi-Nyasa* for Balabhadra and *Kala-Nyasa* for Subhadra are performed. Finally, the *Nyasa Daru* is endowed with life by the *Prana Pratisthita Mantra* a hundred ten times.

On the *Asadha Krushna Charturdashi* night, the *Nyasa Daru* is taken to the temple in a procession in a small *ratha*. It makes seven rounds of the inner *bedha* of the temple and then enters the temple through the *Satapahacha* and *Jaya Vijaya Dwara*, where it is handed over to the *Daitapatis*, who later cut it into four pieces of prescribed size. Each one of these four pieces is used as the lid to cover the *Brahmarandhra* (cavity), in which the *Brahma Pindas* are placed inside each idol. Since the idols also enter the temple on the same night, the entry of the *Nyasa Daru* precedes that.

However, two days before, on the *Dwadashi* night, the *Nyasha Daru* is taken round the inner *bedha* of the temple in a small four-wheeled *ratha* and then brought back to the *Pratistha Mandapa*. This is known as the *Nagara Parikrama*. The premises of the temple is fully cleaned and totally vacated for the purpose like all other cases. The *Nagara Parikrama* is considered as a part of the consecration ceremony.

The Transfer of the *Brahma Pinda*

The newly constructed idols, after completion are taken to the temple on the *Krushna Charturdashi* day at midnight. The idols make three rounds of the inner *bedha* (precincts) in the specially prepared *rathas* one by one (*Pahandi Bije*, in the order of *Sudarshana*, Balabhadra, Subhadra and Jagannath) and enter into the temple through the *Satapahacha* and *Jaya Vijaya Dwara*. They are then placed on the *Anavasara Pindi* (between the *Kalahata Dwara* and the first wooden pole) in front of the old idols.

The process is performed with utmost secrecy and no one, not even the priests of the temple, is allowed inside the temple during the time. Only three *Badagrahi Daitas* and the *Pati Mahapatra* stay inside the sanctum and perform the ritual. Other *Daitas*, who are associated with the process, stay inside the temple but not inside the *Anavashara Pindi* or the sanctum.

The ceremonial transfer of the *Brahma Pinda* takes place on the same night, followed by the sacred burial of the old idols. In order to take out the life substance or the *Brahma Pinda*, the old idols are stripped of their thick coatings two days before the arrival of the new ones, i.e. from the *Dwadashi* day. At the time of the actual transfer, the caskets containing the *Brahmapadartha* are taken out from the old idols and placed in the respective new idols at their appropriate places. The carpenters provide cube-shaped cavity (*Brahmarandhra*) in each idol above the navel and below the left eye with 12 *yabas* of length, breadth and depth, for the *Brahma Pinda* to be placed inside. The transfer of the *Brahma Pinda* takes place in the order (as indicated earlier) of *Sudarshana*, Balabhadra, Subhadra and Jagannath. The *Pati Mahapatra* performs the transfer of *Brahma Pinda* of Jagannath and three other *Badagrahi Daitas* do the job for other idols. Then the cavities of the new idols are securely covered with one of the four pieces of the *Nyasadaru* and the *Bajra Kacheni* is tied. This service is considered as the cream and essence of Jagannath worship. This is also one of the most secret services conducted inside the temple. Even the persons who conduct the service are not allowed to see and experience the event, as their eyes are blind-folded and their hands are also covered with a piece of cloth/robe. Hence, neither they can see it nor feel it. And that is Nabakalebara, the *Brahma Pinda* is transferred from the old idol to the new ones. Then the old idols are discarded and the new ones take their place.

The entire temple is cleaned before the process begins. All the gates and the offices inside the temple are locked, and the keys handed over to the *Daitas*. The *Daitas* take charge of all other temples inside the *bedha* during this period. The *Deula Karana* guards the temple at the *Simha Dwara Gumuta* near the *Patitapabana* image with the *pata khanda* (sacred sword) in his hand. All the lights inside the temple and even outside are switched off so as to prevent people from seeing it even from the neighbouring roof-tops. It is believed that if someone per chance happens to see it, then he is destined to die. The *Daitapatis* perform their work in complete darkness with the help of burning mashals.

What is *Brahma Pinda*?

The *Brahma Pinda* or the Holy Mass representing the Divine Spirit lies in the *Brahmarandhra* of the idols, which are taken out and placed inside the new idols at appropriate places. This mysterious Holy Mass has remained with the idols since the beginning.

Since no one has either seen it or felt it naturally enough, no one can speak with any amount of authenticity as to what is it?. There are quite a number of views about this mysterious object as being Laxmi Narayan *Salagram*, the tooth relic of Buddha, living *Salagram*, the unburnt *Pinda* of Srikrishna, the Golden *Yantra*, parts of the *Daru* of earlier idols, part of the original *Daru* that was floating in the sea at the time of the legendary king Indradyumna, Tantric *yantra* on a metallic plate, a highly precious diamond piece, etc. No authentic view is available in this regard. To sum up all these views, the *Brahma Pinda* is considered as the *Atma* (Life Substance) for the living deity, which has all the features of a human being. The *Daitapatis* associated with it never open their mouth; rather, they express their inability and ignorance in this connection under the pretext of being blind-folded and with hands covered. But whatever it is, two things are certain that once it is placed inside, the new idols acquire the magical power of attracting millions and millions of devotees. The Brahma inside the *Daru* justifies the name *Darubrahma* for Jagannath, the *Daru* *Debata*. The most interesting aspect of the system is that the flowers, the *tulasi*, the *chandana* and the *karpura* that are placed along with the *Brahma Pinda* are said to have remained as fresh as ever at least till the next Nabakalebara. This has been corroborated even by some non-Daitas, who had the scope to obtain some *tulasi* and *chandan* soon after everything was over. This is *Jagatara Nath,* Jagannath, the Lord of the Universe.

The Myth

The whole idea of the *Brahma Pinda* being unseen and unknown seems to be a myth. It can never be accepted that the *Daitapatis* associated with the process have neither seen it nor experienced it. The idea of being blind-folded and the hands being covered with a piece of cloth may be for public consumption, but certainly far from being true. If one sees it from a practical point of view, then different things do come up.

First of all, after the *Brahma Pindas* are brought out from the old *vigrahs,* they are placed on a *khatuli* (small table) in silver pots, known as *Rupabata Bije* and special worship is performed by the *Pati Mahapatra* like *Panchamruta Snana* and *Pankti Bhoga*. The *Badagrahi Daitas* and the *Pati Mahapatra* then apply *chandan, kasturi, karpura, tulasi*, etc., prepared earlier on the *Brahma Pinda*, and place them inside the respective cavities along with some specific white flowers, like *malli, jai* and *jui*. Thereafter, the *Badagrahi Daitapatis* present there pay their respect to the new idols and offer the *Brahma Darshana Bheti* to the Brahma according to their capacity in the form of gold or silver ornaments, cash or other precious materials, which goes to the *Daitapati Niyoga* in due course. All these cannot be performed stealthily in a blind-folded condition.

Secondly, it is not possible to be blind-folded and perform such difficult service. They use sharp weapons like *nihana* and *barishi* to open the navel of the old idols. These must have been very securely fixed. It is quite natural. To be there for more than a decade during which the *Vigrahas* are physically handled and have to move out quite a number of times for *Snana Yatra* and the *Ratha Yatra,* these have to be very tightly fixed to avoid any mishap, which however has never happened so far. Hence, sharp weapons have to be used to open and close the *Brahmarandhras* of the idols. This possibly cannot be performed with blind-folded eyes. Everything has to be accurate and perfect. There is no scope for any mistake or chance. On personal interview one *Daitapati*, associated with the process, chose to remain silent over the issue.

The Experience

Some *Daitapatis*, who have performed the transfer of the *Brahma Pinda* more than once, are still living. When asked about their experience and feeling during the process, they fail to explain it under the pretext that they were blind-folded and their hands were covered with cloth. However, all of them enthusiastically speak of a powerful feeling—the feeling of a supernatural existence. Beyond that there is no other explanation. Whatever may be the truth, whether it is deliberate or divine, the *Daitapatis* concerned have kept it as a closely guarded secret.

The *Daitapatis*, who performed the transfer of the *Brahma Pinda* in the recent past:

Year	*Sudarshana*	Balabhadra	Subhadra	Jagannath
1912	Ramachandra Pati Mohapatra	Hadu Das Mohapatra	Satyabadi Das Mohapatra	Chintamani Swain Mohapatra
1931	Ramachandra Pati Mohapatra	Gadadhar Das Mohapatra	Raghunath Das Mohapatra	Chandra Swain Mohapatra
1950	Ramachandra Pati Mohapatra	Gadadhar Das Mohapatra	Somanath Das Mohapatra	Chandra Swain Mohapatra
1969	Ramachandra Pati Mohapatra	Haladhar Das Mohapatra	Gangadhar Das Mohapatra	Satyabadi Swain Mohapatra
1977	Raghunath Pati Mohapatra	Gangadhar Das Mohapatra on behalf of Haladhar Das Mohapatra	Narasingh Das Mohapatra	Ramakrushna Swain Mohapatra
1996	Raghunath Pati Mohapatra	Haladhar Das Mohapatra	*Bhuban Mohan Das Mohapatra	**Dinabandhu Swain Mohapatra
2015 * Likely to Perform**	Naba Kishore Pati Mohapatra	Haladhara Das Mohapatra	Ramachandra Das Mahapatra	Jagannath Swain Mohapatra

* Sri Biswanath Das Mahapatra was the *Majhi Bada* (the Bada for Subhadra) at that time but Sri Bhuban Mohan Das Mohapatra performed the transfer of the *Brahma Pinda*

** Sri Jagannath Swain Mohapatra was the *Mahaprabhunka Bada* (the *Bada* for Jagannath) at that time but Sri Dinabandhu Swain Mohapatra performed the transfer of the *Brahma Pinda*

*** Under normal circumstances, the above persons are likely to perform the transfer of the *Brahma Pinda* during the Nabakalebara of 2015.

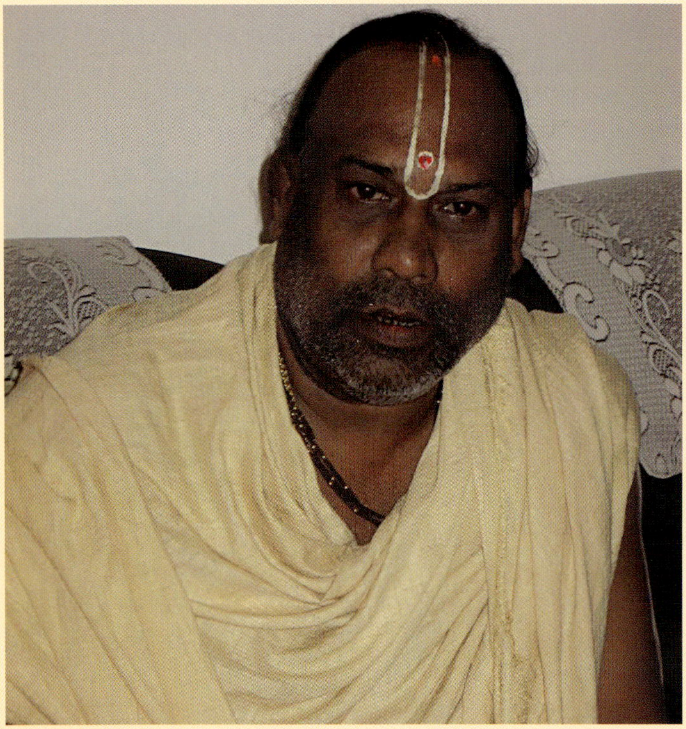

Facing page (No. 56):

Top left:
67. Jagannath Swain Mohapatra, the *Mahaprabhunka Bada* (Bada for Jagannath).

Top right:
68. Haladhara Das Mohapatra, the *Bada Bada* (*Bada* for Balabhadra).

Bottom left:
69. Rama Chandra Das Mahapatra, the *Majhi Bada* (*Bada* for Subhadra).

Bottom right:
70. Raj Kishore Das Mohapatra, the *Biswabasu* 1996.

This page:

Left:
71. Naba Kisohre Pati Mohapatra, the *Pati Mahapatra*.

Centre:
72. Chandan Hajuri (standing), the *Deula Karana* with Rajkishore Das Mohapatra.

Right:
73. Haladhar Das Mohapatra, the *Bada Bada Daita*.

The Sacred Burial

After the transfer of the *Brahma Pinda*, the old idols are considered as dead. The *Daitapatis* carry them in the same *rathas* in which the new idols were brought and bury them under the *Siali Lata* (*Bauhinia Bauhinia Vahlii*) in the *Koili Baikuntha*, the graveyard of the Lords before dawn. This is called *Patali* or *Golak Bishram* of the Lords. This *Golak Bishrama* of the idols is comparable to the final end (*Ananta Bishram*) of Sri Krushna under the *Siali Lata* after being struck by the arrow of Jara Sabara.

74. The *Golaka Bishram* of the Lords under the *Siali Lata* at *Koili Baikuntha* (painting).

A big pit of 9 *hata* (approx. 4 ½ metres) deep and 6 *hatas* of length and breadth is dug by the *Kotha Suansia sevakas*. A red velvet cloth is spread on it, after which the discarded idols are buried there. The *Sudarshana*, the *Sarathi* and the *Parswa Devatas*, the *Apsaras*, horses of the *rathas* and all their used materials like cloths, beds, pillows etc. are also buried there.

It is believed that if anyone other than the *Daitapatis* sees the burial, he is destined to die. Hence, no one, not even from the roof-top of the nearby buildings, should happen to see it even by chance. As such it is not possible for anyone from outside to see it because the pit is covered with thick grove of *siali lata* permanently. The government, however, declares full black-out of the entire town during the night.

The entire atmosphere is charged with a feeling of remorse and deprivation. The people feel bereaved as if someone from their own family or someone very near and dear to them has passed away. The *Daitapatis* associated with the burial fail to control their tears. They have been physically and emotionally associated with the idol for years, which is now being discarded. A sense of gloom prevails over the entire town. The day following the burial brings the entire town to a standstill. There is no movement or merrymaking all around. A melancholic situation prevails over the town. Their beloved and highly revered deities are gone and they are yet to see the new ones.

The *Daita* and the *Pati Mahamapatra* families, as the relatives of Lord Jagannath, observe funeral rites and remain in ritual impurity (*asaucha*) for 10 days from the night of the burial as they claim Jagannath to be their relation and one of their clan. They observe it as if someone from their family has expired. After the burial, the *Daitas* go for an oil massage near the Jhulanamundi and then leave the temple through the *Simha Dwara* to take bath in the Markanda Tank. Then they re-enter the temple through the *Simha Dwara* and take the *Shantiudakka* near the *Mukti Mandapa*. Their wet cloth is taken by the *Dhoba Sevaka*. During the following 10 days, they observe all the obsequies of the funeral rites as per the Hindu system. On the tenth day, all the members of the *Daita* and *Pati Mahapatra* families cut their nails, shave themselves and take a purificatory bath in the Markanda Tank. Their houses are white-washed and all their family members put on new dress, supplied by the temple administration. On the *Trayodashi* day, as a part of the twelfth day observation, thousands of Brahmins, saints, pilgrims, common people, etc. are served with *Mahaprasad*. The *Daitapati Niyoga* takes care of the expenses. As a matter of fact, the funeral ceremony was observed by the *Daitapatis* in 1996 from 16.06.1996 to 26.06.1996.

As a normal hereditary law, the survivors inherit the property of the deceased. Hence, the *Daitapatis* also lay their claim to the property of Lord Jagannath. They are normally compensated in the form of cash by the temple administration but the most important are the relics of the old idols like sandal paste, cloth stripes, flowers, etc., which are eagerly sought after by the devotees.

Besides the funeral observations by the *Daita* and the *Pati Mahapatra* families, normalcy rcturns from the second day to the temple as well as the town. People start visiting the temple and await the *Nabayauban Darshana*.

The difference between the regular *Ratha Yatra* and that of the Nabakalebara Year

Ratha Yatra is an annual festival. However, some difference is marked in the *Ratha Yatra* of the

Bottom:
75. Preparation of *Ratha* in progress.

Top right:
76. Skeleton of *Ratha* without cloth covering.

Centre right:
77. Jagannath being dragged during *Pahandi*, tied with ropes.

Bottom right:
78. *Pahandi* of Jagannath.

Preceding page (No. 61):

Top left:
79. *Pahandi*, tied with ropes, the Pata Dori.

Top right:
80. *Pahandi* of Balabhadra.

Centre left:
81. *Pahandi* of Balabhadra.

Centre right:
82. *Pahandi* of Subhadra being carried on shoulders.

Bottom left:
83. Paintings of the *Sakhis* for the *Rathas*.

Bottom right:
84. *Parsvadevatas* for the *Rathas*.

This page:

Top:
85. *Parsvadevatas* - Nandighosh, the *Ratha* of Lord Jagannath.

Centre:
86. *Parsvadevatas* - Taladhwaj, the *Ratha* of Lord Balabhadra.

Bottom:
87. *Parsvadevatas* of *Darpadalana*.

Facing page (No. 63):

Top:
88. Preparation of horses for the *Ratha*.

Bottom left:
89. Preparation of parrot for the *Ratha*.

Bottom right:
90. Preparation of *Sarathi* for the *Ratha*.

91. A view of the *Rathas*, ready to be pulled.

92. Nandighosha, the chariot of Jagannath, leaves the main temple.

93. Three *Rathas* in front of Sri Mandir.

Facing page:
94. Three *Rathas* in front of Sri Mandir.

vedanta
SHRI
ANNATH
LE OFFICE

95. *Suna Besha* of Lord Jagannath on the *Ratha*.

96. *Suna Besha* of Balabhadra on the *Ratha*.

normal years and that of the Nabakalebara year. Every year all the three *Rathas* are prepared afresh but the *Sarathis* of all the three *Rathas*, all the horses, the *Parswa Devatas*, the *kalasas*, the brake wood and few other items are retained as such without any change. This is repeated year after year but during the Nabakalebara year, everything is changed. This is a natural necessity as some of these items like the *Sarathis*, the horses, the *Parswa Devatas*, etc. are buried along with the idols in the Sacred Burial. Hence, there is need for the preparation of completely new *Rathas* including all the components, meaning thereby Nabakalebara of the *Rathas* as well. As such, the

Top:
97. *Suna Besha* of Subhadra on the *Ratha*.

Top right:
98. Naba Kishore Pati Mohapatra along with other *Daitas* on the *Ratha*.

Centre right:
99. *Suna Besha* on the *Ratha*.

Bottom right:
100. *Suna Besha* on the *Ratha*.

Ratha Yatra gives an opportunity to one and all to pay their devotional respect to the new idols. Unlike other festivals, during the *Ratha Yatra* the *Chaturdha Murty* come out of the temple in their own wooden form to give an opportunity to different categories of people, even people from different religions, to see the gods. No priest intervenes and people freely embrace the idols. The *Ratha Yatra* is the only occasion when people of other religions get to see the gods. On all other days of the year, they are supposed to satisfy themselves by seeing the *Patitapabana* image near the *Simha Dwara*. As a matter of fact, every year thousands of non-Hindus, and more so the foreigners, attend the *Ratha Yatra* to have a *darshana* of the Lords. This becomes all the more necessary after the Nabakalebara, as that becomes the first *darshana* of the new idols. Hence if five lakh plus people turn up for the usual *Ratha Yatra*, more than fifteen lakh are expected for the Nabakalebara *Ratha Yatra* of 2015.

Select Bibliography

Basham, A.L., *The Wonder that was India: A Survey of the History and Culture of Indian Subcontinent Before the Coming of the Muslims*, New York, 1968.

Behera, K.S. , H.S. Patnaik, M.P. Das and R.K. Mishra (ed.), *Charles Grome's Report on the Temple of Jagannath,* Bhubaneswar, 2002.

——, *George Webb's Report on Jagannath Temple,* Bhubaneswar, 2003.

Bhandarkar, R.G., *Vaishnavism, Saivism and Minor Religious Systems*, Strassburg, 1913.

Das, A., *Nabakalebara*, Cuttack, 1969.

Das, M.N., *Glimpses of Kalinga History*, Calcutta, 1949.

Das, S., *Jagannath Mandira O' Jagannath Tatwa*, (Odia), Cuttack, 1982.

De, S.C., "The Cult of Jagannath"*, JKHRS,* Vol. I and II, Bhubaneswar 1947.

Eschmannn, A., H. Kulke and G.C. Tripathy, *The Cult of Jagannath and the Regional Tradition of Orissa*, New Delhi, 1978.

Giri, P.N., *Jagannath O' Nabakalebara*, (Odia), Cuttack, 1996.

Khuntia, C., *Nabakalebara* (Odia), Puri, 1996.

Khuntia, S., *Nabakalebara Tathya Samikhya* (Odia), Puri, 1969.

Kulke, H., *Kings and Cults,* New Delhi, 1993.

Mishra, B., *Nabakalebara of Shri Jagannath, Puri,* Bhubaneswar, 2013.

Mishra, J.K., (Tr.), *Bamadeva Samghita* (Odia), Puri, 2008.

Mishra, K.C., *Jagannath and Nabakalebara*, Puri, 1969.

——, *The Cult of Jagannath*, Calcutta, 1971.

Mishra, P.C., *Shri Jagannath Darshan*, (Odia). Cuttack, 2008.

Mohanty, B.M. (ed.), *Shrikhetra Sri Jagannath* (Odia), Cuttack, 1986.

Mohanty, G., A.K. Pattanayak, *et.al.* (eds.), *Cultural Heritage of Odisha, (*Sri Jagannath Special Volume), Vol. XII, Puri Dist. (Part III), Bhubaneswar, 2010.

Mukherjee, P., *History of the Jagannath Temple in the 19th Century*, Kolkata, 1977.

Nayak, A., *Jagannath Parba Parbani* (Odia), Cuttack, 1999.

O'Malley, L.S.S., *Bengal District Gazetteers*: *Puri*, New Delhi, 2007.

Padhi, B.M., *Daru Debata*, (Odia), Cuttack, 1964.

Patnaik, A., *Mahadebata*, (Odia), Cuttack, 2010.

Roy, B. (ed.), *Chariots Divine*, Kolkata, 2012.

Stirling, A., *An Account: Geographical, Statistical and Historical of Orissa Proper or Cuttack*, Calcutta, 1822.

Swain, B.K., (Tr.), *Niladri Mahodiya* (Odia), Vol. I and II, Puri, 2007.

Tripathy, G.C., "Nabakalebara, The Unique Ceremony of The Birth and Death of The Lord of the World", in A Eschmann (ed.), *The Cult of Jagannath and The Regional Tradition of Orissa,* 1978.

——, *Communication with God: The Daily Puja Ceremony in the Jagannath Temple*, New Delhi, 2004.

Tripathy, M., *Shri Jagannath*, Bhubaneswar, 2013.